Protecting Your Assets

A Cybersecurity Guide for Small Businesses

John A. Schaefer

EASTVALE
PUBLISHING
AN EASTVALE SOLUTIONS COMPANY

For more information, please contact:

Eastvale Publishing
330 Franklin Road, Suite 135A-130
Brentwood, TN 37027
www.eastvalepublishing.com

ISBN 978-1-950353-00-2

To Susan

For knowing how to keep me focused.
For calling BS when necessary.
For making me take breaks and watch hockey.

But most of all, for believing in me.

Table of Contents

5

CHECKING THE BOXES 59

6

A STRUCTURED APPROACH 71

7

CONTINUING THE JOURNEY 81

A

GLOSSARY 89

B

ENDNOTES 101

EMBRACE THE GREY

Congratulations on taking a proactive step to increase your awareness and understanding of the biggest threats facing small businesses today. I am, of course, talking about cybersecurity.

Yes, I said it. Cybersecurity. Now take a deep breath and relax. There's no need to go running for your happy place, because cybersecurity isn't something to be afraid of. It's when you don't have it that you should be worried.

I'm sure you've already figured out that this isn't going to be your typical book on the topic. First, it's written in the first person. I've found it's easier to have a conversation than to lecture or judge. Second, I am a computer geek - but please don't hold that against me. While I've had a long and varied career with Information

Systems and Information Security, I've also learned a lot of non-geeky things along the way.

I have a passion for learning and sharing what I've learned. And I have the ability to take technical topics and present them in such a way that they're understandable and relatable by normal people that aren't necessarily technical. (Yes, I just implied that geeks aren't normal - and I'm standing by that assertion.)

As an example, I'm sure we've all seen news reports or read articles about cyber attacks by bad guys. These stories usually have an expert that tells you exactly what you *need to do* or things that you *must never do* to stay safe and secure. You'd think from listening to these reports that we live in a black-and-white world, and that cybersecurity is a one-size-fits-all proposition.

It's a lie.

Do they know your line of business? Do they know the risk tolerance of your organization? There is no one-size-fits-all solution for cybersecurity. Every organization is different - the type of data, appetite for accepting risk, visibility as a target, and many other considerations go into creating a secure environment. Cybersecurity isn't black-and-white. I'm here to help you learn to embrace the grey areas.

This book will assist small businesses in getting a better handle on cybersecurity. Yes, there will be lists - because there are some fundamental things that everybody should be doing. It's not unlike changing the oil or rotating the tires on your car; preventive maintenance is part of the cost of ownership.

HOW LONG HAS THIS BEEN GOING ON?

Early adopters of the Internet as a business tool gained a competitive advantage over those with a wait and see attitude. While it took a leap of faith to make that move 25 years ago, those businesses were rewarded with a fertile market whose potential few could envision at the beginning. As an example, Amazon.com was started in 1994 as an online bookstore and was based in Jeff Bezos' garage.[1] In their 2017 fiscal year, Amazon.com sales were just shy of $178 billion.[2]

Finding success is more difficult on the Internet today, but there are still examples such as Airbnb, Lyft, and Houzz. These types of companies are referred to as *disrupters* because they challenge long established business models They are also examples of something called a *digital business*.

The term digital business has been around for a few years, but there is still disagreement on the exact meaning of the term. When I use the term, I mean "A digital business is one that uses technology as an advantage in its internal and external operations."[3]

I may be cheating a little, because this definition means that nearly every business today is a digital business. But in all honesty, there are very few companies that don't use computers or the Internet for at least some part of their operations. Whether it's simply maintaining a website, conducting sales, or communicating with suppliers, it's nearly impossible to conduct business today without using computers or technology to our advantage.

Even setting aside the Internet, computers allowed companies to be more efficient, better manage inventory and resources, and reach a global audience that wasn't possible until recently.

Like most things, though, there is a darker side to these advancements. Cybercriminals can break into unsecured computers and create chaos. Whether it's depleting bank accounts, creating fake online orders, or encrypting your information and demanding a ransom to recover it, the bad guys can attack from anywhere in the world with an Internet connection. Younger generations, who've never known a world without these technologies, have an inherent trust in all things digital - which is also used by cybercriminals to their advantage.

There continues to be a prevailing misconception that cybercriminals are awkward teenagers living in their parent's basements. But that's an outdated stereotype. The real threat today comes from professional hackers-for-hire, organized cybercrime organizations, and nation-state sponsored activities.

These groups are structured like any other organization. They are well funded, use cutting edge technology, and tend to attract some very talented individuals. In 2017, 50% of all successful attacks were carried out by organized criminal groups.[4] Based on current trends, cybercrime will cost over $6 trillion annually by 2021.[5] That's more than the illegal drug trade in the entire world combined. Forbes even refers to these cybercrime organizations as the modern-day mafia.[6]

The bad guys invest in technology to make them more effective and ruthless. The interconnected nature of the modern world means the attackers can be anywhere in the world. And technology is advancing at such a rapid pace that the number of devices keeps growing, frequently with vulnerabilities that can easily be exploited.[7]

In his TED talk, James Veitch brilliantly observed that "The internet gave us access to everything; but it also gave everything access to us."[8] And it's never been easier to get access to everything, because most people now carry a super-computer (laughingly called a smart phone) in their pocket.

Cybersecurity is a never-ending process. It's a journey and not a destination. New vulnerabilities continue to be found, and attacks are constantly evolving. Anything that documents specific risks will become outdated quickly. The truth is that the bad guys only need to be right once, cybersecurity defenses need to be right 100% of the time to stop them.

That's not realistic.

So how are small businesses supposed to protect themselves from these types of sophisticated operation? Believe it or not, there are actually some relatively simple things that any organization can do to improve their security posture.

THE FORGOTTEN MAJORITY

First off, why focus on small businesses? Why should you, as a small business owner, care about cybersecurity? Well, it gets down to being a numbers game.

First, the 2018 Verizon Data Breach Investigation Report (DBIR) found that 58% of all cybercrime victims were small businesses.[9] Second, small businesses are an important part of most national economies.

According to the US Small Business Administration (SBA), there are over 30.2 million small businesses in the United States. Small businesses are responsible for nearly half of all private-sector output and almost two thirds of all new jobs.[10] In the United Kingdom (UK) at the beginning of 2018, 99.3% of all organizations were small businesses and accounted for more than half of all private sector revenue.[11]

Starting and running a small business is difficult enough, with little guarantee for success. In the US, about 20% of small businesses will fail in their first year and roughly half fail by five years. The numbers for the UK are slightly lower initially, but are similar in the long run.

Because most small businesses are focused on producing products and gaining customers in order to survive, many tasks not related to their core business is done as a *best effort*. Cybersecurity is typically one of those activities, if it's considered at all. The National Institute of Standards and Technology summarizes the situation nicely:

> *For some small businesses, the security of their information, systems, and networks might not be their highest priority. However, an information security or cybersecurity incident can be detrimental to their business, customers, employees, business partners, and potentially their community. It is vitally important that each small business understand and manage the risk to information, systems, and networks that support their business.*[12]

So What Exactly is a Small Business?
Like I've already mentioned, small businesses play a very large role in the economies of the US, UK, and EU, but it holds true for

most developed countries. But what exactly is considered a small business?

Unfortunately, it's not a simple discussion. The main reason is that the US Small Business Administration (SBA) doesn't have a single definition. Instead, it's based on either annual revenue or the number of employees, and those numbers vary by industry.

Compare that to the European Union (EU), which defines a *small enterprise* as having less than 50 employees and less than €10 million in annual revenue or €10 million in assets. There's an additional category referred to as *micro enterprises*, which are those with less than 10 employees and less than €2 million in revenue or assets.[13]

The UK defines micro and small enterprises by the same employee counts as the EU, but without the asset or revenue restrictions.[14]

These distinctions are important and really drive home just how vital Small and Micro businesses are to the global economy.

There is a lot of information targeted towards and available to medium and large companies, who generally have more personnel and financial resources available to put towards cybersecurity. Meanwhile, smaller organizations are usually lumped together with either home users or with medium businesses, neither of which really address their needs.

Misconceptions

There also seems to be a belief in the broader cybersecurity community that small businesses aren't worth the time or effort. This in turn leads some small businesses to believe they don't need to invest in cybersecurity.

That vicious cycle of neglect leading to denial has caused a lot of churn and some misconceptions, even among cybersecurity professionals.

To make matters worse, there are some technically minded people who believe they're better or more intelligent than non-geeks. Many thrive on FUD - Fear, Uncertainty, and Doubt - using worst-case examples and doomsday scenarios to try and convince others of their viewpoint. From my observations, these same individuals also use a lot of Generalities and Exaggerations, so what you really end up with is FUDGE!

This behavior is especially prevalent among people selling cybersecurity products or services. Many will try to scare or intimidate small organizations with FUDGE, saying your business must have their widget or risk being overrun by bad guys. Then there's the other end of the spectrum, where they believe that small business = small sales, so they never even reach out to smaller organizations to see what their needs are.

But the fault isn't exclusively with cybersecurity professionals or vendors. Many small businesses continue to believe that they're too small for cybercriminals to bother with or that they don't have anything worth stealing.

Easy Targets

The truth is that, due to sheer numbers and lack or cybersecurity investment, small businesses are easy targets. The belief that small organizations don't have anything worth stealing shows a lack of understanding about the cybercriminal mindset. Every computer has some value to the bad guys, which typically comes in two forms.

The first is the information that the computer potentially contains. This can be intellectual property (that thing that makes your company unique, which for a bakery can include something as simple as Grandma's secret pie recipe), customer and employee information (names, addresses, and more), financial information (yours or that of your clients), your future product plans, and a list so long it could fill an entire book by itself. Any information you have on your computer or accessible from a cloud service provider (like Dropbox, Microsoft Office 365, or SalesForce.com) can be valuable.

The second value is from the computer's processor and storage itself. Once they have access to a computer, cybercriminals can remotely install malware like viruses and ransomware. And because today's computers have more processing power than most users need, this extra capacity can be used by the malware without the user's knowledge or awareness.

The bad guys are able to combine the processing power from hundreds, or even thousands, of computers running their malware to create something called a botnet (short for robot network).

These botnets can be instructed to carry out attacks that disrupt access to a website or try to break into a system. There are cybercriminals in the bad neighborhoods of the Internet who control botnets and sell their processing power to others as a service. Anything with a processor, from computers to security cameras to appliances that connect to the Internet, can potentially become part of a botnet.

The Implications

Think of it this way. What would you do if you couldn't get to information stored on your computer? How long could your organization continue to operate without access to email? Or to your customer records? What about to your orders or inventory? What would happen if your website were defaced or hijacked?

Some small businesses would be able to continue for a while. A bakery would probably be okay, assuming they can still get to Grandma's recipes. But what happens when they run out of ingredients? Can they place an order via the phone or do their suppliers only take orders online?

For a more technology dependent organization, such as an online retailer, the impact is felt immediately. If they can't take or receive orders, their revenue stream just stopped. Unless they can repair the damage, their future is in jeopardy.

These examples highlight why the one-size-fits-all approach I mentioned in the introduction doesn't work. Not every small business has the same risks, and therefore can't treat cybersecurity the same way. The bakery may be able to survive in an *analog* mode for months, where the online retailer may only have a few hours before irreversible damage is done.

The Domino Effect

Sometimes the information the bad guys steal has secondary or tertiary value, which may not be obvious at first glance. The information about your organization is certainly valuable, and probably what you think of first. But does your organization have data about your customers or their activities that the bad guys can use?

Customer names, addresses, credit card information, and purchasing history can also be extremely valuable. Attackers have been known to impersonate employees of organizations from which they've stolen information, trying to steal from their customers as well.

In a recent real-world scenario, a customer of a company I'm calling *15 Petals* was contacted about making a payment for something they were purchasing. The caller knew their names, details of the purchase, and other information that only someone from 15 Petals should have known. In this case, the customer was personal friends with the owner of 15 Petals, and became suspicious about the way the caller pestered them for the credit card verification (CCV) number from the back of their card. Pretending not to have their card handy, the customer told the person they'd need to call back - and then contacted their friend.

Because 15 Petals follows the Payment Card Industry (PCI) Data Safeguarding Standards (DSS), they don't store the CCV number. Whoever stole the customer information could get the CCV, but they had plenty of other information. The bad guys then used social engineering to try and get customers to give up their CCV numbers. If they were successful, they could have then made purchases with the stolen card data.

This wasn't the only instance. 15 Petals has determined that somehow certain customer information had been stolen. It's still unclear if the breach occurred within their organization or one of their suppliers, but the investigation is on going.

IT'S JUST A BUNCH OF WORDS

WARNING! Technical Content! This chapter may seem a bit geeky or technical for some readers. However, it's essential to have a common understanding of some key terms in order to have a productive discussion. I promise to make it as painless as possible.

Information technology, and especially cybersecurity, has a unique vocabulary that may be unfamiliar to people outside of the field. There are words that have very specific meanings, which may differ or be more nuanced than those used in everyday conversations.

This chapter provides information needed throughout the rest of this book. I'm not going to get into the weeds, and you don't have to have an in-depth understanding of the terms. However, knowing the difference between a threat and a risk will make the rest of the book easier to digest. There's also a glossary with additional definitions for other terms I use in the book.

Privacy, Security, and Anonymity

The words *security* and *privacy* are frequently used interchangeably, but they are not the same thing. There's also a third component that people don't generally think about, which is *anonymity*. The three are related, but each has a it's own unique meaning.

Security can be thought of as *Freedom from Danger*. This can be interpreted in many different ways, depending on the situation. For example, the local police and fire departments are a form of security. When it comes to computers, security can mean running an operating system resistant to attack, using anti-malware software, not running as a local administrator, and not visiting bad neighborhoods on the Internet.

Privacy is *Freedom from Observation,* essentially meaning you can do something without someone else watching. Things that you do in your house with the blinds closed are generally private. It's more difficult to have privacy on a computer, where certain websites or operating systems assume you want everything to be public unless you say otherwise. (Just look at Facebook if you have any doubts.)

Lastly, **Anonymity** is best described as *Freedom from Identification*. Someone can watch you do something, but you can remain anonymous if they don't know who you are. In our modern, interconnected world, anonymity is very difficult to achieve. There are thousands of trackers, widgets, and beacons that collect and correlate information from millions of websites.

And despite being different, they are three very important concepts, especially when it comes to things you do to protect your customers and your organization. If you collect any type of personally identifiable or credit card information from customers, their privacy needs to be protected by your security. Likewise, your organization's privacy policy should do everything it can to protect the anonymity of your clients.

Cybersecurity

Using the definitions above, it's pretty easy to see that cybersecurity is more focused on protection from danger than anything else.

Before getting into the nuances, however, I need to air a bit of dirty laundry. You may have seen cybersecurity written differently in other books and publications. That's because there's still disagreement among some security practitioners on how cybersecurity should be written, especially in different English speaking countries. The US favors it as one word - cybersecurity - while the UK and EU seem to prefer it be written as two words - cyber security. There's even a middle-ground variation that throws in a hyphen - cyber-security. For our conversation, I'm going to use cybersecurity as one word for a couple of reasons. First, it's become the standard spelling for most government organizations, including the National Institute of Standards and Technology (NIST). Second, it's the way the Merriam-Webster, Oxford, and Cambridge English dictionaries all spell it.

For our purposes, **Cybersecurity** means the practice of protecting computers and the information they contain from being attacked, stolen, or compromised. This is achieved through an understanding of risks and threats, and ensuring that appropriate countermeasures are in place. The definitions that follow are all directly related to cybersecurity and are necessary to understand the discipline in its entirety.

Confidentiality, Integrity, and Availability

One of the basic tenets of cybersecurity is the concept of Confidentiality, Integrity, and Availability (CIA) for things that are essential for an organization. These *things* are collectively referred to as **Assets** - and will be different for every industry, and even vary from organization to organization. While data regulated by state or federal governments is typically an essential asset, your organization may also have product designs, customer databases, or some other information that's vital. Assets also include computing hardware and software, manufacturing or production equipment, employees, and other things that are vital for your organization to continue functioning.

Confidentiality is ensuring that only authorized individuals have access to information, and inadvertent disclosure is prevented - typically through systematic controls. Confidential information can be anything that your organization deems vital to your continued operations and success.

Integrity relates to information and computing systems themselves. Integrity means ensuring that information is true and accurate, that any changes to data or system configurations are authorized, and that controls are in place to detect or prevent unauthorized changes.

The last leg of the triad is *Availability*, which essentially means you can access the information you need whenever you need it.

If any one of these pillars fail, it affects the other two. For example, information that is kept confidential and has validated integrity is of little use if it can't be accessed. Likewise, information that is available and verified can be problematic if it's disclosed to the wrong people.

The concept of *Non-Repudiation* is occasionally bundled in with the CIA triad, but it's predominantly used as a legal term. It's meaning for cybersecurity relates to proving that a transaction occurred and was legitimate. It's not integral to the concepts discussed in this book, and is included here simply for completeness.

Threats, Vulnerabilities, and Weaknesses

The next set of terms have to do with items that can impact the CIA triad: threats, vulnerabilities, and weaknesses. These terms are yet another example of words having specific meanings. They're also frequently confused with risk, which we'll discuss later in this chapter

Threats are external factors that can impact information systems and cover a wide gamut. Disgruntled employees, cybercriminals, natural disasters, malicious software (malware), industrial espionage, and a whole litany of other factors are all potential threats.

Vulnerabilities are different from threats in that they're deficiencies within a system or process. Vulnerabilities are capable of being exploited or are open to attack, and are generally beyond our direct control. An example would be something within an operating system (such as Windows or Android) that can be taken advantage of by an attacker. There is nothing the we can do to directly fix these vulnerabilities. We have to wait for Microsoft or Google to release a patch for us to apply. (There are indirect things that we can do to protect against vulnerabilities that we'll address under the topic of risk.)

The idea of **Weakness** is closely related to vulnerabilities. Weaknesses are flaws in the design or implantation of a system. The difference between a vulnerability and a weakness is that we can directly address a weakness. Examples of weaknesses are misconfigured firewalls, unpatched systems, or lack of documented procedures within an organization.

Countermeasures, Impact, and Risk

Every organization, even those engaged in cybercrime, wants to do whatever they can to prevent bad stuff from happening to them. **Countermeasures** are those things that an organization can do to minimize the impact of a threat. Locking your car doors when you park is an example of a countermeasure. In the cybersecurity realm, countermeasures include things like firewalls, anti-malware software, and having a strong password policy (all of which are discussed in The Inevitable List).

For our purposes, **Impact** means the effect on an organization if a *threat* exploits a *vulnerability* or *weakness*. In other words, what's the consequence of having the confidentiality, availability, or integrity of your computer systems compromised?

All of these build up to the discussion of risk, which is itself a multifaceted topic. **Risk** can be defined as the threat posed to an organization based on potential threats, the impact if that threat is realized, and the likelihood of it happening. It can be represented as a mathematical formula and is easily measured.

The formula below is one generally accepted way to calculate any type of risk, not just cybersecurity risks.

$$Risk = \left(\frac{(Vulnerability + Weakness) \times Threat}{Countermeasures} \right) \times Asset\ Value$$

For this formula to be useful, however, you need to understand the variable and their values in order to assess the risk. This isn't a one-size-fits-all exercise, and will differ between industries and companies. How much risk an organization is willing or able to tolerates will differ greatly. And, just to make it more interesting, risk changes over time and needs to be reassessed on a regular basis. Like I said, security is a journey.

Risk Appetite and Risk Tolerance

This is really what everything discussed in this chapter comes down to. Your organization will need to decide for itself how willing or able it is to accept risk, or spend money to reduce the risks.

The amount of risk that any given organization is willing to accept is referred to as their **Appetite for Risk**, and it's going to depend on a number of things. Is your organization highly regulated, like a financial institution? If so, you may be compelled by legislation to have a lower risk appetite than a company in a different industry.

Risk Tolerance is about the uncertainties - living in that grey area I mentioned before. The higher your organization's risk tolerance, the more willing you are to take risks and absorb losses. In cybersecurity terms, that means being willing to spend the time, effort, and money required to stop the bleeding, tighten your security posture, and live with the consequences after a successful attack has occurred.

There is no such thing as perfect security. Something bad is eventually going to happen. Going in with your eyes open and knowing what you're willing to lose before something bad happens will allow your organization to better prepare for it, absorb the impact, and get back to business faster.

THE INEVITABLE LIST

Regardless of an organization's line of business, there are some basic steps that should be taken to protect computing assets. You've probably seen a number of lists like this (I know I have); but they usually don't provide any context or details. They're usually just, well, a list.

This chapter showcases some simple things your organization can do that will dramatically increase its cybersecurity, many at little or no cost. Incorporating these essential components into your normal business processes will greatly increase your organization's cyber resilience and pave the way for the more advanced methods and techniques discussed in the chapter on the NIST Cybersecurity Framework (NIST CSF). Many of these are also required for compliance with various laws or regulations.

I'm not trying to say "Do these things or else your business is doomed". Like I said before, I don't know what your organization does - and I believe every organization is unique. If your organization has done a risk calculation and identified your risk tolerance, some of these items may not be worth the time. On the other hand, if you haven't done the calculation or your tolerance for risk is low, then I'm recommending this is where you should start.

1. Change All The Defaults

Nearly every piece of hardware or software comes configured with default accounts, passwords, or names for the devices. That's convenient if you forget the factory setting or lose the manual, because a quick Internet search will tell you what they were. But that also means that cybercriminals have collected these settings for nearly every system and device manufactured in the past 20 years, and will always try them first. It's like leaving the combination lock on your luggage set to *000* and assuming no one's going figure it out.

Changing the defaults is a simple, no-cost way to improve the security for any organization. But it's something so simple and obvious that it can sometimes be overlooked, even for large organizations. Remember the Target breach of 2013? The one that cost them $292 million?[15] It was determined that it was caused by default passwords being used on some devices.[16]

2. Require Passwords

Passwords is one of those topics I find difficult to discuss. It's not because it's a difficult topic, but it's one I've been talking about for over 30 years. And sometimes it gets frustrating.

There are studies done every year that look at the most common passwords that have been leaked online. The 2018 SplashData study found the two most common passwords are (still) 123456 and password[17], ranking #1 and #2, as they have since 2013.[18] While using any of the passwords on their list needs to be avoided, to see these topping the list five years in a row is disheartening.

Passwords aren't flashy or exciting, and I know they never will be. I don't know of a single person who's happy when they need to change their password, myself included.

Passwords have been problematic since their inception. The concept of passwords date back to MIT in 1961. They had a large computer that was shared by numerous people. Each user was assigned a password they used to access the system, which enforced usage quotas. The first problem was that there were no user IDs - just passwords. The second problem was that the passwords for each user were stored on the shared system, in plain text, and available to everyone. It took less than a year from the creation of the password for someone to hack the system. All they needed to do was print all of the passwords, and then login as other people when their own time allotment was used up.[19]

Instead of scrapping the password system, however, they just kept changing it. First by encrypting the passwords, then by adding user IDs, and then by giving users the ability to select their own passwords. But those were just enhancements to a flawed system that continues to be troublesome. Even today, there are some systems that don't require complex passwords or that allow unlimited password guesses without locking out the account.

These continued weaknesses are one of things that the bad guys count on. They use custom-built computers designed solely for trying to break into systems. We use the term *brute-force*, which is a pretty accurate description, since they're able to try tens of thousands of guesses a second. These systems also have lists of billions of potential passwords, called *rainbow tables*, that include every possible combination of letters, numbers, and special characters up to 12 characters long. And if the system they are attacking doesn't limit the number of login attempts, they can keep trying until they are successful.

The reason for 12 characters has to do with the way passwords are stored. I'm not going to go into the technical details, but passwords longer than 12 characters are stored differently than those 12 characters or less. If an attacker is able to copy a directory of user IDs and passwords, it's much easier to crack shorter ones.

So, in a nutshell, we're still living with the consequences of a defective system designed more than a half century ago.

Biometric authentication (finger prints, facial recognition, retina scans, etc.) is finally becoming mainstream, but it's not available on the majority of devices yet. So passwords are going to remain a necessary component of cybersecurity for the foreseeable future.

Passwords and biometrics fall into the category of authentication - which is how you prove to the system or device that you're you. A correct combination of user ID and password (for computers) or password, fingerprint, or face (for smart phones and tablets) and you're allowed in.

You may have heard that there are some rules that you need to follow for passwords. Endorsed by the majority of cybersecurity practitioners, these "rules" generally don't make people happy or make things any simpler. I generally don't agree with them because, in most cases, they're not realistic. If more people embrace the realities I describe below, it will make passwords a little easier to deal with.

Generally Accepted Passwords Rules

Rule #1: A strong password is long (at least 13 characters) and contains upper and lower case letters, numbers, and special characters.

Reality #1: A good password is one that only you know and can remember, but that would be impossible for anyone else to guess. One of the problems is simply that we call them pass*words*. Most systems today will accept a whole lot of characters, so we shouldn't limit our thinking to just words. We need to start thinking about pass phrases - combinations of words that are easy to remember (and type).

Randall Munroe showed this concept in his XKCD comic from August 10, 2011.[20] (Just don't use his example as an actual password.)

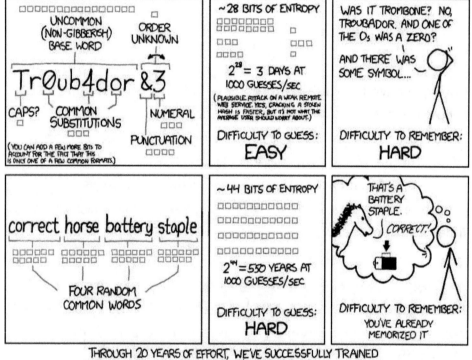

THROUGH 20 YEARS OF EFFORT, WE'VE SUCCESSFULLY TRAINED EVERYONE TO USE PASSWORDS THAT ARE HARD FOR HUMANS TO REMEMBER, BUT EASY FOR COMPUTERS TO GUESS.

WARNING! Technical Content! Entropy refers to the lack of order or predictability for any set of information. In the case of passwords, entropy is calculated as a^b, where "a" represents the number of possible values (letters, numbers, symbols, etc.) and "b" is the length of the password. For those interested, explainxkcd.com goes into quite a bit of details regarding the math.[21]

Another problem with complex password rules is that people tend to pick convenience over security. They believe that they're being clever when they substitute a symbol for a letter or number. But I can guarantee you that bad guys know all of these tricks and more. As noted by Paul Grassi with NIST,

> *Everyone knows that an exclamation point is a 1, or an I, or the last character of a password. $ is an S or a 5. If we use these well-known tricks, we aren't fooling any adversary. We are simply fooling the database that stores passwords into thinking the user did something good.[22]*

There are several sites on the Internet to test password strength, and most will indicate how long it would take to crack. I prefer the site howsecureismypassword.net for its simple interface and realistic calculations. (If you type the password from XKCD into the site, you'll see why I said not to use it. It's so well known, it's in every rainbow table in existence.)

Rule #2: Passwords need to be changed every three months.

Reality #2: Back when passwords were limited to six or eight characters, that was probably good advice. Should you change your passwords? Absolutely! Does it need to be quarterly? Probably not.

Sure, you could use a 34 character password that the testing site says would take an average of 20 quindecillion years to crack. (That's 20 followed by 48 zeros). But if you change your password on an annual basis, a 13 character password that could be cracked in 50 years is perfectly fine. And it's easier to remember.

The goal isn't for your password to remain unbroken until the end of time. The goal is for your password to remain unbroken until the next time you change it.

Rule #3: A different strong password needs to be used for every system you use that requires authentication.

Reality #3: The main argument for this approach is that passwords from previous breaches are available on the Internet, and a lot of people reuse one password for nearly everything. I'm not a believer in this approach because it treats your banking or social media accounts the same as enthusiast forums or blogs. Not every system or device contains something of value, so why should we protect them all the same way? Why do I need a password to sign into web forums, or newspaper sites, or any number of other places that don't store information that needs to be secured? Logins for these sites are really only for tracking purposes and to target advertising. I believe that a tiered password system is more realistic and easier to manage.

Tier 1 - Strong, Unique Passwords Required. This applies to passwords for your organization's systems, for banking and investment sites, or anywhere else where Personally Identifiable Information (PII) is stored. Email also falls into this category, because if your email is compromised, then the bad guys can request password resets and get them via your emails - so all bets are off. Under no circumstances should these passwords be the same, because if one of the sites is compromised then the bad guys have access to everything. Some would argue that social networking sites would fall into this category, and there certainly is an argument to be made for that. Basically, if there's a genuine risk of losing something of value (monetary, reputational, emotional, and personal things can all have value), then it deserves to be protected appropriately.

Tier 2 - Any Password Will Do. This is for the sites I mentioned before (forums, blogs, news sites, etc.). These passwords don't protect anything critical, and are really just used to make sure you've signed-up to have access to the content. This pretty much applies to any website where your personal or credit card information isn't stored. Even some pay content (like newspaper sites) would fall into this category, as long as your credit card number isn't stored. Any password could be used for these sites, since there's an extremely low impact if the password is compromised.

Rule #4: Passwords should never be written down.

Reality #4: Passwords should never be written down on sheets of dead trees, with or without sticky stuff on the back. Even if adobe a tiered system, there will still be a lot of passwords that you need to remember. So why not use technology to help you tame technology? By that, I mean you should be using an electronic wallet (aka, password store). There are many different products to select from, and the features vary from product to product. Some are only for passwords, while others let you secure all your sensitive data. Some let you synchronize the information between computers, tablets, and smartphones, while others store your information in the cloud for access from a browser. Some of the more popular products are 1Password, Dashlane, KeePass, and LastPass. I personally use eWallet from Ilium Software. They're a much smaller company, but their product has better features than most of the big players in the space. (And no, I'm not getting anything for this or any other endorsement in this book.)

Rule #5: Passwords should never, under any circumstances, be shared.

Reality #5: Passwords should never, under any circumstances, be shared. If someone knows your account name and password, they can impersonate you. They can post as you on social media, buy stuff as you from online stores, even change your passwords to lock you out of your own accounts. Since they used your real user ID and password, you'll have a very difficult time proving that it wasn't actually you that did all those things.

3. Use Multi-Factor Authentication When Possible

A *factor* is something that contributes to the production of a result (like logging into a computer).[23] There are generally three categories of factors when discussing cybersecurity:

- something you know (like your password)
- something you have (like a 1-time password generator or an authenticator app)
- something you are (like your fingerprint).

When you login to a system or device with a user name and password, it's considered single-factor authentication (1FA). You use your user name plus something you know -your password - to authenticate yourself.

Multi-factor authentication (MFA), also known as two-factor authentication (2FA), two-step verification (2SV), and several other similar terms, adds something else to the mix. While these terms all refer to something slightly different, at their core they mean that you need your user name plus two things when you login to a service or device. MFA is a great security measure because it's nearly impossible for a cybercriminal to get access to both of the things needed to login. Even if they have your password, they can't login without the other piece - either something you have or something you are.

The *de facto* standard for MFA interoperability is FIDO U2F (Fast ID Online Universal Two Factor), and championed by the FIDO Alliance[24]. With over 240 members,[25] it's one of the largest technology collaborations focused on cybersecurity that exists.

For major computer operating systems (mac OS, Windows, and most versions of Linux), MFA compatibility is built-in to the currently selling version. For the "something you have" component, you'll generally need to purchase a device compatible with FIDO U2F. While Yubikey is the best known brand, there are other manufacturers. A complete list of USB authenticators can be found on the FIDO Alliance website.[26] This same device can also usually be used for securing access to websites, and some versions will even secure mobile devices (tablets and smart phones) that support Near-Field Communications (NFC).

The options for MFA on mobile devices is more limited. Devices running Android or iOS have some good security features built into them, but lack other controls. One example of this is devices that allow access with a fingerprint or facial recognition. That's technically still only 1FA (something you are). While significantly better than a password, it will never be as secure as using MFA with those devices that can support it.

Many popular websites already offer MFA capabilities, but it's amazing how few individuals take advantage of it. Amazon, Apple, Dropbox, Facebook, Google, LinkedIn, and Zoom are just some of of the companies that offer some form of MFA, but you have to take proactive steps to enable it. Some will send a text message to an enrolled device, some have an authenticator application you need to download from an app store, and others support FIDO devices. Regardless of the method, it's worth the effort to enable this feature whenever possible.

4. Keep All Software Up-To-Date

Just like there's no such thing as perfect security, there's also no such thing as perfect software. Every application ever written has had a flaw or *bug*.[27] While not every flaw is related to security, the good majority are.

The ubiquity of vulnerabilities is such that there is a list published every week that contains vulnerabilities and exposures reported in the last seven days.[28] Called the Common Vulnerabilities and Exposures (CVE) database, each vulnerability is given a criticality score based on the severity and how easy it is to exploit. And since this list is publicly available, the bad guys can (and do) use it to build their own databases of what to look for when they attack a system.

When vulnerabilities are discovered, manufacturers generally publish patches or updates to resolve these vulnerabilities for versions of their software that are still supported. These patches are free to download and install, and in most cases are available before or soon after the CVE is published. However, there are still organizations that don't patch their systems.

Remember the 2014 Sony breach? It was caused by exploiting a weakness known as SQL Injection - which had been around since 2002![29]

Another important aspect of keeping software up-to-date is making sure you're running a *supported version* - which means that the manufacturer still offers updates and patches. The older software gets, the more likely that new vulnerabilities will be found - usually something critical. If the software is no longer supported, then no patches will be created to fix the vulnerability.

The amount of time that software is supported varies widely between manufacturers. As an example, Windows XP was released in August 2001, and support for it ended in April 2014. Twelve years is a great run for any operating system, but it could no longer support newer hardware being sold. Some people still haven't given up on it, however. At the end of November 2018, over 4.23% of all computers on the Internet were still running Windows XP. What's truly amazing, however, is that this is up from 3.16% at the end of September 2018.[30] Since it was discontinued, over 50 significant vulnerabilities for Windows XP were reported in the CVE - none of which will ever be patched by Microsoft.

It's really this simple: Upgrades are a cost of doing business. Not upgrading could cost you your business. It's no different than replacing a piece of equipment for which you can no longer get parts.

5. Use Anti-Malware (Anti-Virus) Software

Malware, a melding of Malicious Software, is an overarching category of programs that includes computer viruses, ransomware, spyware, and other nasty software designed to damage your computer and/or steal your information.

The first computer virus was released in 1971.[31] Computer pioneer John von Neumann, however, had theorized about self replicating programs in the 1940s and wrote about the concept in 1966.[32] While the concept and first instance of viruses were purely theoretical, modern malware is anything but that.

One of the first large-scale malware outbreaks was the ILOVEYOU virus in 2000. It was spread through an email attachment and was able to infect over 45 million computers in the first 24 hours.[33] Since then, large scale malware outbreaks have occurred every few years; the most recent being the WannaCry ransomware attack in 2017.

Despite no major outbreaks in 2018, there were roughly 10 million new pieces of malware released every month, bringing the total number to over 856 million.[34]

Anti-malware software is an essential piece in any organization's cybersecurity arsenal. When kept up-to-date, new virus definitions are added on a daily basis to provide a first level of defense against the bad guys. Also, malware affects more than

Windows these days. Android, MacOS, and Linux all have had malware written against them and need to have an anti-malware product installed.

> **WARNING! Technical Content!** Anti-malware software relies on signatures to identify malware. This means that it can only stop something that it knows about. Anti-malware software is far from perfect. However, when used as part of a larger cybersecurity arsenal, it's an essential component for protecting against known threats.

As of December 2018, Apple's iOS is the only operating system that hasn't had malware released against it *in the wild*. There has been some proof-of-concept malware created and tested academically, and there were some NSA tools uploaded to WikiLeaks. There have been viruses written for jailbroken devices, but a regular iPhone or iPad is by far the most secure device currently available. This is reinforced by the fact there is no anti-malware software available for iOS.

The features and capabilities of the different anti-virus products continue to evolve and leap-frog each other, so it's difficult to recommend a specific product. However, the website av-test.org compares all of the major anti-malware vendors on a regular basis and provides easy to understand reports. This information should help your organization select the product that best meets your unique needs.

6. Limit Access to Systems and Devices

I will admit it's possible that every employee in your organization needs to have administrator access to every system - but you have to admit that it's highly unlikely. Unless you're a sole proprietor, there are going to be systems that some of your organization's employees shouldn't be able to access - like payroll systems or bank accounts.

Limiting access to just those systems or devices that an employee needs to do their job is called the *principle of least privilege*, and it's a great way of isolating the damage that can be done to your organization. If everyone can access everything, all an attacker needs to do is compromise one person and they have access to everything. The same applies if you have a disgruntled employee who wants to harm your organization. Without the principle of least privilege, they already have all the access they need to steal intellectual property, delete critical information, or otherwise wreak havoc.

Role-Based Access

One way to effectively implement least privilege access is to identify the roles within your organization. These should already exist with most organizations, either as job descriptions or merely assigned tasks. However, the more formal the descriptions, the easier it is to translate them into the access needed for any given system or device. If your organization doesn't currently have defined roles, this is a perfect time to implement them - and take care of two issues with a single effort.

As mentioned earlier, every industry and organization will have different roles with different responsibilities, so I can't really provide more specific guidance.

Limit Local Accounts
There is, however, another aspect of limiting access that's frequently overlooked, and it has to do with the accounts you use on your computer.

Does the account you use day-to-day on your computer belong to the local administrator group? Why? Administrative access is typically only needed to install new software or perform some very specific tasks, but the majority of computer users run as administrators all of the time.

When you buy a new computer, the user name that you pick during the setup process will automatically be an administrator. It takes some extra work to create a normal or power user account, but the benefits are worth the effort. This doesn't apply to Android or iOS devices because their operating systems are fundamentally different, but it should be done for all Windows, MacOS, and Linux computers.

The bad guys know that most people will pick the convenience of running as an administrator over the security of having to occasionally switch accounts. In fact, they count on it because it makes their lives easier.

That's because the majority of malware has historically required administrator access in order to install itself. While this is changing as attacks get more sophisticated, the vast majority of the 856 million pieces of malware mentioned earlier can't run without administrative user permissions. This obviously isn't fool proof since there are still millions of pieces of malware that could potentially infect your computer, but it increases your odds greatly.

7. Create Separation of Duties

This is related to limiting access, but has to do with who is authorized to perform certain tasks within your organization. Separation of Duties (SoD) means that more than one person is required to complete certain tasks. For example, the ability to implement security settings within a system and the ability to audit and verify those security settings should be assigned to different people. Allowing one individual to have total control of a given process can compromise cybersecurity controls.

SoD is not just a good cybersecurity practice, either. There are certain regulations, such as the US Gramm-Leach-Bliley Act (GLBA) and the EU's General Data Protection Regulation (GDPR), that mandate SoD for certain functions. Proper separation can also prevent conflicts of interest, which further helps to meet compliance requirements. While this may not apply to some micro businesses, it's something that needs to be considered by a significant number of organizations.

8. Secure Your Files

One benefit of computers and the modern way of working is being able to share information between individuals, making organizations more efficient and agile. But just like limiting access to systems and devices enhances security, so does limiting what people can do within systems and devices. While securing files and limiting access may appear to be the same thing, let me give you an example to help illustrate the difference.

If your organization has 10 employees, perhaps you want to give them all access to your HR system. This would allow them to see their personal information, submit hours, view benefits, and a myriad of other possible tasks. That's appropriate access to the system. But should every employee see information about other employees? Probably not. Only your HR employees should have that level of access. Everyone else should only be able to get to their own information.

Private employee and HR information typically needs to be protected for legislative reasons, as does any customer information you may need to keep. If it's not properly protected, it can lead to non-compliance and It's also likely that access to financial and banking information should be limited.

Your organization's other files and data may also need to be secured. Should Grandma's recipes be available to everyone? Maybe. But what about your organization's plans for future products or production schedules? If this type of information is compromised, it can put you at a competitive disadvantage if it were made available to your competition.

9. Backup Your Data

Backups are one piece of a broader Business Continuity / Disaster Recovery topic discussed later in this chapter. Having backups directly relates to how quickly an organization can recover from an incident. Whether it's a cyber attack, natural disaster, or just a lost laptop, not being able to access certain data could be disastrous for some organizations. In order to provide the most comprehensive level of protection, many security practitioners, myself included, recommend the 3-2-1 approach for backing up data.

3 - Have at least three copies of your data - the original and two backups.
2 - Have your data on two different devices. In other words, don't create a backup of your data on the hard drive of your computer that has the original.
1 - Make sure that one copy of your data is offsite or in the cloud.

The reason to use two different devices is to ensure you can still get to your data if your hard drive crashes or your computer is stolen. The reason for an off-site copy is to protect against a natural disaster or some other catastrophe. It's typically recommended that offsite copies be stored at least 50 miles from the original to ensure that a natural disaster doesn't affect them.

This guidance was reinforced by Hurricane Harvey and the Paradise, CA, fires of 2018.

Also, at least one of the devices used for backups (USB hard drive, thumb drive, networked storage, file server, Internet backup, etc.) should only be connected when actually creating the backup. This is to guard against ransomware - malware that encrypts data and demands payment to unlock it. If all your backup devices are connected when the ransomware encrypts your data, the backups will also be encrypted and therefore become useless.

10. Turn on Encryption

Encryption is a process of taking data and transforming it so that it's no longer readable by a human. While encryption can be used for nefarious purposes like ransomware, it can also be used to protect your data from attackers. I'm not going to go into the mechanics of how encryption works. Suffice it to say that if the bad guys can't read your data, it's of no value to them.

For mobile devices like smartphones and tablets, simply creating a lock screen password will typically also enable encryption for the device. Some Android phones and tablets have removable storage (SD-cards) that need to be encrypted separately from the device.

Computers running Windows, MacOS, or Linux typically require additional steps to turn on encryption, and those steps will vary based on the manufacturer and the version of the operating system.

Most online services encrypt data automatically, but this should be confirmed with your provider. In addition, ensure that your online service provider uses a different encryption key for each client and not one common key for everyone.

If they're unable (or unwilling) to answer these basic questions, it may be time to look for a new solution.

11. Educate Employees

Or, if you're a sole proprietor, educate yourself. Cybersecurity isn't the most entertaining topic to learn about, but it is essential. And, if I do say so myself, reading this book is a fantastic start. Employee eduction can be delivered in many different ways (in person, online, required reading of written materials, etc.), but all training should cover the same basic topics. Let your employees know:

- what laws and regulations your organization must abide by
- that everyone in the organization has a responsibility for cybersecurity
- your expectations for their conduct relating to information, systems, and devices
- your process for reporting suspected incidents or weaknesses they may discover

Each of these is a broad category that can include a lot of details, but the content needs to be tailored for your industry and organization. As Entrepreneur magazine notes, "there is no such things as sharing too many tips on security with your staff".[35]

There are an amazing number of training resources available to small businesses to help with employee awareness. In the US, NIST, the SBA, and a number of other agencies have content that can be used as-is or offer guidance for creating your own materials. The Stay Safe Online and Stop-Think-Connect initiatives, while aimed at individuals, also have resources for small businesses to be better informed and educate their employees. The UK has the National Cyber Security Centre (NCSC), which is part of the GCHQ office, while the EU has a number of resources available through the ENISA website. These are all fantastic sites offering training topics and ideas at no cost.

For organizations looking for ready-to-go training materials, there are a number of companies that provide generic cybersecurity training - but these may be cost prohibitive for smaller organizations.

12. Have Written Policies and Procedures

Most organizations think of personnel related topics when thinking of Policies and Procedures. And while health and safety, harassment, code of conduct, and a number of other policies are vital, many organizations don't include cybersecurity policies in their HR handbooks. In order to best protect your organization, there are a minimum of three policies that you should implement to reduce your cyber risk.

- **Device Use Policy.** This would cover two topics. First, what is permissible to do with a device (computer, tablet, or phone) that you provide to your employees? Are they allowed to use them for personal things? Conversely, are your employees permitted to use their personal devices to conduct business? The goal of both of these topics is to ensure that your organization and data are properly secured and accessed.
- **Internet / Email Policy.** Here is where you document what is acceptable from the web browsing and communications standpoint. Should you allow employees to visit bad neighborhoods on the internet? This includes not only pornographic or gambling sites (which could lead to harassment or code of conduct violations), but also bomb making, hate-speech, and terrorist sites. Are they allowed to use company email for personal use? How should they handle messages that have unsolicited ideas for your organization, make legal demands, or claim to be from suppliers?
- **Social Media Policy.** Since most social media platforms allow users to list their employers, anything your employees post on their personal pages can reflect badly on your organization and have a negative impact. It's because of this negative blow-back that it's appropriate to have a policy on the topic. Banning your employees isn't realistic (or even legal, in most cases), but you can provide guidance so that they state their posts are their opinions, that they aren't speaking for your organization, or some other similar language. You may also want to assign a

couple individuals that are authorized to maintain your organization's social media accounts and post on your behalf.

These polices all relate to company assets being provided to conduct company business. Industries such as financial services and healthcare have regulatory requirements that their policies must address, which may make them stricter than those in a manufacturing or consulting organization.

Larger organizations typically have technical controls in place to enforce their policies. Tools such as device management software and content filtering firewalls allow them to prevent unwanted activities from occurring, but these are controls that smaller organizations rarely have the luxury of implementing.

13. Business Continuity Planning and Disaster Recovery

"If you fail to plan, you are planning to fail" is a quote famously attributed to Benjamin Franklin. I prefer an updated version of this sentiment from Alan Lakein, "Planning is bringing the future into the present so that you can do something about it now."[36] Regardless of which you prefer, they both highlight the need to be prepared in case some bad things happen to your organization.

Business Continuity Planning (BCP) and Disaster Recovery (DR) are frequently discussed together because they are really two sides of the same coin. BCP (also called disaster planning) is the up-front work to anticipate the worst-case scenarios that can impact your organization, while DR (also called business resumption) is the work needed after the bad stuff has happened in order to get back to business.

It's too late to think about this after a disaster has occurred. BCP is about having a plan laid out ahead of time to deal with difficult situations, hoping that you'll never have to invoke your recovery plan.

A BCP should realistically use your risk calculations and consider the impact of each threat to the day-to-day operations of your organization, not just those related to cybersecurity. The list below includes some of the disruptions that need to be considered in your BCP.

- Loss of a Facility or Inability to Reach a Facility
- Loss of Key Employees
- Loss of Infrastructure (roadways, electricity, landline/cell phone, water/sewer, etc.)
- Loss of Supplier or Supply Chain Disruption

Of course, there are some cybersecurity specific items that should also be included.

- Denial of Service Attack Against Your Organization
- Defacing or Hijacking your Company Website
- Compromise of Your Bank Account or Financial Systems

- Inability to Access Your Organization's Data
- The loss of your Computing Capabilities

The 1987 Whittier Narrows earthquake was an eye-opening event for many companies in the Los Angeles basin, and provides a real world example of just how vital BCP activities are.

First Interstate Bancorp (now Wells Fargo) revised their continuity and recovery plans after the earthquake to account for the wide-wide-speed effect of such a natural disaster.

Then, on May 4, 1988, there was a fire at their headquarters building in downtown Los Angeles that destroyed five floors. This mostly affected their securities trading business and it could have been catastrophic. However, their BCP included sending backups to a different location and allowing their securities brokers to keep certain information on floppy disks. Fire sprinklers weren't required when the building was constructed, but the BCP identified this risk and plans were already underway to retrofit the building. Because of these precautions, the overall impact of the fire was minimal.[37] As far as their customers were concerned, it was business as usual on May 5th. While there was information lost, it could have been significantly worse.[38]

Now think of your own organization. Would you be able to recover from this type of disaster? How long would it take? Would our customers wait until your organization was back up and running?

14. Secure all Webpages, not just Login or Checkout

If your company has any type of Internet presence, this is something that you need to do now. For many years, it was thought that only web pages that collected sensitive information (passwords, credit card data, etc.) needed to be encrypted (typically denoted by HTTPS instead of just HTTP in your browser). This, however, is no longer the case.

Google announced a change in release 68 of their Chrome browser. Any webpage not using HTTPS would now be labeled as *Not secure* by the browser. So why should you care? Chrome's marketshare as of December 2018 is over 60%,[39] meaning that nearly two thirds of people visiting your website will be told your site is insecure. This alone may be enough for your customers to take their business elsewhere.

Google appears to be on a one-company crusade to raise the security of the entire Internet, and that's not necessarily a bad thing. Regular HTTP is vulnerable to a number of attacks, including content spoofing (inserting false information into the page a user sees) and sniffing (reading the information transmitted between the browser and webpages).

But wait, it gets worse. Several high profile vulnerabilities discovered in 2014 exposed issues with existing encryption standards of HTTPS. Dubbed *Heartbleed* and *Poodle*, these exploits exposed vulnerabilities in some core Internet technologies.

> **WARNING! Technical Content!** HTTP is the HyperText Transport Protocol. It's what allows content to be displayed in your web browser. HTTPS is the Secure version of HTTP, using encryption to protect the information sent to and from your browser from being visible to everyone else. HTTPS originally used a protocol called Secure Sockets Layer (SSL). In Internet terms, SSL is ancient - having originally been introduced in February 1995, with an update in 1996.
>
> An enhancement to the protocol, called Transport Layer Security (SSL-TLS or just TLS), was introduced in 1999, with updates in 2006 and 2008. Version 1.3 of TLS was officially defined and ratified in 2018. As discussed below, due to some serious vulnerabilities with earlier versions, TLS 1.2 and 1.3 are the only secure versions of HTTPS.

All versions of SSL and version 1.0 and 1.1 of TLS are vulnerable to these attacks, meaning that most of the information sent over HTTPS was no longer secure. Only TLS 1.2 and 1.3 are secure, meaning anything else will also cause Chrome to flag a website as *Not secure*.

This is relevant to cybersecurity because any data not secured by TLS 1.2 or later can potentially be intercepted, read, and manipulated by cybercriminals - which can impact all three triads of the CIA pyramid. It puts not only your organization at risk, but also any information that your customers may provide via your website.

If you're using a third party company to develop and maintain your organization's web site, they should have taking care of this for you already. It's easy enough to check by viewing your web site in the Chrome browser and, if it's *Not secure*, making sure your provider takes care of it immediately.

If your organization maintains their own site, then this is something the employees who manage your site need to fix.

15. Firewalls & Internet Security

I mentioned in the policy section that tools to filter Internet content or manage devices are luxuries for most small businesses, especially since simply surviving the first few years can be a challenge. There are, however, some basic controls that every organization should have in place.

Many small businesses use consumer-grade Internet service, usually for cost savings. With this type of service the device you get from your Internet provider is usually just a modem that allows you to connect. It is not a security device and it cannot protect your computers or network. In order to provide basic protection, you'll need at least a router. If your organization is using consumer-grade Internet service, a consumer grade product should also be sufficient.

A device that has a router, a firewall, and WiFi integrated into one device may be all you need. A lot will depend on how large your facility is (and if you have more than one), how many employees you have, and how much you need the Internet for your business.

If your organization is using a business-grade Internet solution, bear in mind that these services and the hardware needed to utilize them are typically *a la carte*. Unlike products aimed at consumers, most small business routers don't include wireless (WiFi) capabilities. Some small business offerings even remove firewall functionality from the router, meaning you need to purchase up to three different products.

Unfortunately, this isn't one of those topics where I can provide more specific advice about the design of your network or what devices are required. What I can tell you is the same thing from the first topic - change the defaults. And I'm not just talking about the administrator name (if possible) and password.

For WiFi networks, there are a few items that need to be configured or changed. This first is something called the Service Set Identifier (SSID) - which is the name of your WiFi network to which your computers will connect. Make it something unique to your organization so that it's easily distinguishable, but don't bother trying to hide it. There are some WiFi devices that allow you to "hide" the SSID so that it's not *visible* or *broadcast*, but hiding the SSID does not mean it's secure. All it means is that it will take hackers a few extra seconds to find it.[40] Hiding the SSID is also a violation of the wireless networking standard, meaning that it's likely some devices won't connect to a hidden SSID.[41]

The second has to do with WiFi security and, depending on your wireless access point, there can be numerous choices. Similar to the situation with SSL discussed in the previous section, there are some WiFI protocols that are no longer secure. WiFi also has the option of having no security - which is typically the default value. With no security, anyone with any device can access your network and, in most cases, connect to every other computer.

The minimum security needed is called WiFi Protected Access v2 with Pre-Shared Key (WPA2-PSK). The pre-shared key is the password you need to enter the first time that you connect to the network. If your organization has a technical staff, you may be able to use WPA2 Enterprise, which uses certificates instead of the pre-shared key.

> **WARNING! Technical Content!** A word of caution, however. Even WPA2 has a known weakness, as was documented in CVE-2017-13077 through 13082 ,CVE-2017-13084, and CVE-2017-13086 through 13088.[42] While the WPA3 standard has been finalized and ratified, devices adhering to the standard only began shipping in late 2018. It will take years for all device to support the new standard, so this is something we're going to have to live with for a bit longer. All that being said, WPA2 is still significantly better than having no security at all.

One last thing to configure is turning off remote management over the Internet, especially if you're using a consumer-grade device. There were some vulnerabilities discovered in 2016 that allowed the bad guys to take over routers across the Internet and potentially access and steal data that's being transmitted on the network.

Case Study: WannaCry Ransomware

I know that there was a lot of information to digest in this chapter, but I want to highlight how some of these simple changes can have a big effect.

In May 2017, malware called WannaCry started infecting computers around the world and began encrypting their information. It spread from one computer to another across networks, passing on its payload before encrypting that computer as well. WannaCry was well publicized and could have been a lot worse had security researchers not found a kill switch that disabled the virus.

WARNING! Technical Content! WannaCry exploited a vulnerability in a piece of the Windows operating system called the Server Message Block (SMB). This vulnerability was known to the Central Intelligence Agency (CIA), details of which were published on the Wikileaks web site earlier in 2017. Known as Vault 7, there were a number of other CIA hacking tools revealed at the same time. So how was WannaCry able to encrypt over 200,000 computers in 150 countries in just a few hours? One reason is that a lot of organizations don't take care of the cybersecurity basics I talked about in this chapter.

Keep All Software Up-To-Date
Microsoft released a patch in March 2017 that plugged the hole used by WannaCry. It couldn't run on systems that had the patch installed.

Also, Windows 10 isn't typically vulnerable to WannaCry because SMB was disabled by default. Something that many people have also forgotten is that Windows 10 *was free!* At least it was free for the first year. WannaCry would have done much less damage if more people had taken advantage of this free update.

Limit Access and Create Separation of Duties
If the principle of least privilege were more widely used, it would have been possible to slow the spread of WannaCry and limit its overall impact. Ransomware can't encrypt what it can't access. By only giving employees access to systems and devices they need to do their jobs, you're also limiting the impact of the malware.

Backup Your Data
By having a backup that's not connected to the computer all the time, it would have been possible to restore the infected systems with minimal effort.

Business Continuity Planning and Disaster Recovery
Lastly, having a BCP would have allowed organizations to identify the threats posed by an attack like WannaCry. While it may not have prevented them from becoming infected, they could have invoked their recovery plan quickly and easily.

CHECKING THE BOXES

The basic safeguards discussed in the previous chapter apply to every organization, whether or not they're engaged in a regulated industry. And while not every small business has to comply with governmental regulations, the majority have to deal with at least some form of oversight.

Compliance ≠ Security

The supposed reason for a lot of industry-specific legislation is to ensure a common level of security between organizations. Recent history, however, has shown that being compliant and being secure are two very different things.[43] Target, Home Depot, The UPS Store, Sally Beauty, Sonic Drive-In, and numerous other large organizations had compliance certifications and were still successfully attacked.

Because of this phenomenon, many cybersecurity professionals refer to compliance as checkbox security. I disagree. Security and compliance are different and need to be treated as such. I've already mentioned that the goal of cybersecurity is to protect confidentiality, integrity, and availability. The goal of compliance, on the other hand, is to satisfy regulatory or industry-specific requirements.

I think I've driven home the point that cybersecurity isn't one-size-fits-all, but compliance is - at least for companies that have to abide by certain laws and regulations. If you think of it this way, then having a checklist that you can follow for compliance isn't a bad thing at all.

To put it another way, compliance is what you *have to do*, while cybersecurity is what you *should be doing*. There's typically going to be some overlap, but the amount is going to vary based on the laws and regulations with which a particular organization needs to comply. Think of it like this:

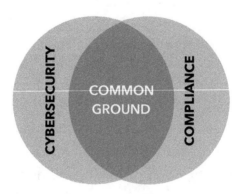

Organizations that have a fully formed cybersecurity program will generally find it simpler to achieve compliance. There will certainly be additional requirement, but it's not like starting from scratch.

The Tangled Web of Privacy Laws and Regulations

Privacy is the category that most people think of when it comes to regulations, probably because it casts the widest net. It's the one that I'm going to focus on, because nearly every organization has some type of private information that they need to protect.

Privacy laws generally deal with *Personal Data* (also referred to as *Personally Identifiable Information* (PII)), but this is where it begins to get messy.

There are over 80 different national privacy laws around the world.[44] And the types of information that constitutes personal data vary greatly from country to country.

Location, Location, Location
These differences matter because privacy laws are based on the citizenship or residency of the individual whose personal data your organization may have, not where your organization is located. If you have personal data about an EU citizen or resident, it doesn't matter if you're is located in Frankfurt, Germany, or Lebanon, Kansas; GDPR still applies to you.

As you're reading this, you may think you don't have anything to worry about because your organization isn't in the EU and neither are your customers. But that's where you can run afoul of GDPR, because it applies to EU *citizens*, regardless of where they live.

To illustrate just how convoluted privacy compliance can become, we'll look at another real-world example. An elderly couple immigrated to the US after World War II have lived in California since the 1950s. They have social security cards, paid US taxes for 70 years, and lived in the same house since the early 1970s. She's active in the local social scene, and he retired from a large multi-national organization more than a decade ago. From all outward appearances, a successful couple enjoying their golden years. If they do business with your organization, you'd never suspect you might need to take extra precautions with their personal data.

But things aren't always as clean cut as we'd like. You see, for various reasons, this couple didn't become US citizens. They're permanent residents (aka, Green Card holders) and have EU passports. By definition, EU passport = EU citizen - which entitles them to all the protections dictated by GDPR.

Because they live in the US, their healthcare providers must comply with the Health Insurance Portability and Accountability Act (HIPAA) requirements and their financial institutions must adhere to the Gramm-Leach-Bliley Act (GLBA). And because they live in California, state privacy laws would apply as well.

European Union

There was a lot of buzz in early 2018 about GDPR - the EU General Data Protection Regulation.

Despite being adopted in 2016 and taking effect in May of 2018, there still seems to be confusion about GDPR from organizations outside of the EU. But the scenario above should serve as a reality check that every organization should at least have a basic understanding of what GDPR entails.

At its core, GDPR gives individuals control over their personal data - calling it a "fundamental right".[45] It also prescribes how organizations need to protect the information they have about individuals. The information defined as personal data is lengthy, including such things are identification numbers, GPS location information, computer serial number or Internet Protocol (IP) address, and anything specific to an individual's "physical, physiological, genetic, mental, economic, cultural or social identity", and more.[46]

With its broad definition of personal data, GDPR actually begins to blur the lines between privacy and anonymity.

Under GDPR, all data being acquired by an organization from or about an individual must be disclosed. In most cases, consent must be obtained for its usage. GDPR gives individuals extraordinary visibility and control of their personal data, including the right to request the following.

- What data an organization is collecting about them.
- Why an organization is collecting the information.
- How long the information will be kept.
- With whom the organization will share the data.

Organizations have to respond within 30 days of of receiving the request. Individuals also have the right to correct information about themselves that they discover is inaccurate or incorrect.

The most talked about aspect of GDPR, however, is the *Right to be Forgotten*.[47] Individuals have the ability to withdraw consent, which means organizations may have to delete information they have about an individual if requested. There are exceptions to this right (such as data still needed for legal obligations), but it gives a lot of power to individuals to control how their data is collected and used.

Brazil

It may seem odd that I'm including Brazil in this list, but it's here for two reasons. First, it's one of the most recent national privacy laws, having been enacted in August 2018. Second, it has some unique things defined as personal information.

Known as the General Personal Data Protection Act , it goes into full effect on August 15, 2020.

Among the items defined as personal data are ethnic origin; religious beliefs; political opinion; membership in trade unions, religious, or political organizations, sexual orientation, genetic information, and more.[48]

United States

Noticeably absent from the list of countries with comprehensive national privacy laws is the United States. There are instead some industry specific regulations and an uneven coverage at the state level. This has led to over 100 different privacy laws at the state level - including 25 for California alone.[49]

Because many of these laws have different definitions of personal data, it's difficult to know what would constitute a breach should data be stolen.

California Consumer Privacy Act
The State of California passed legislation modeled after GDPR. Officially called the California Consumer Privacy Act of 2018 (CCPA), it's usually referred to as California GDPR because of how similar it is to the original.

The law, which took effect on January 1, 2019, has 12 categories of personal data. As you can see from the partial list below, the items that need to be protected is longer and more comprehensive than GDPR.

- Identifiers such as a real name, alias, postal address, IP address, electronic mail address, account name, social security number, driver's license number, passport number, or other similar identifiers
- All categories of personal information relating to race, ethnicity, or gender
- Commercial information, including records of property, products or services provided, obtained, or considered, or other purchasing or consuming histories or tendencies
- Biometric data
- Internet or other electronic network activity information, including but not limited to, browsing history, search history, and information regarding a consumer's interaction with a website, application, or advertisement
- Geolocation data
- Audio, electronic, visual, thermal, olfactory, or similar information
- Psychometric information
- Professional or employment-related information
- Inferences drawn from any of the information identified above[50]

While that's a lot of information, there is a silver lining. CCPA has minimum requirements that shield many small businesses. Most organizations with less than $25 million in gross annual revenue are exempt from the provisions. Only organizations that receive, buy, or sell more than 50,000 consumer records, or that earn more than 50% of their annual revenue from selling personal data need to comply.[51]

Tennessee Identity Theft Deterrence

In the State of Tennessee, personal data is only called out for deterring identity theft, and only includes an individuals' first name or initial and last name, plus any of the following

- social security number
- driver's license number
- bank account or credit card number with the security code.[52]

This disparity between California and Tennessee illustrate just how different state privacy laws are from each other.

US Healthcare Regulations

Healthcare is one of the areas where the US has a national privacy standard. In fact, it has two of them.

The first of these is HIPAA, which deals with the privacy and safeguarding of medical information. It was enacted in 1996 to standardize how medical record information is shared. HIPAA was updated in 2013.

The second is the Health Information Technology for Economic and Clinical Health (HITECH) Act of 2009, which encouraged the use of electronic health records, the adoption of technology standards, and testing of information systems.

While HIPAA and HITECH are separate laws , they do reinforce each other. In fact, HITECH specifically states that standards and technology it mandates will not compromise HIPAA. Conversely, the 2013 HIPAA update adopted breach notification rules similar to those in HITECH.

US Financial Regulations

Owing to various financial scandals of the past, the financial industry is one of the heaviest regulated in the US. When it comes to privacy, however, the Gramm-Leach-Bliley Act (GLBA) is the primary regulation.

Passed in 1999, GLBA requires financial institutions to explain how they share and protect the PII of their customers. It defines financial institutions as companies that offer financial products or services such as loans, financial and investment advice, or insurance.

One shortcoming of GLBA is that it lacks a clear definition of personal data. It instead uses the term *nonpublic personal information* and broadly defines it as information an individual provides to the financial institution that cannot be found elsewhere.

As you can tell, compliance becomes complex very quickly. And that's just the privacy laws!

I obviously can't cover every possible scenario as it relates to personal data, but I can offer some general guidance.

- Understand where your organization has physical locations and where you conduct business.
- If you collect any information from your customers, you need to understand if it's defined as PII by their place of residence or citizenship.
- It's not realistic to protect personal data differently based on the locations of your customers. Therefore, strive to comply with the strictest regulations that apply to your organization.
- Don't assume that encrypting personal data will protect you in the case of a breach. Not all locations have safe harbor provisions or reciprocity.

WARNING! Technical Content! Safe harbor refers to a legal provision to reduce or eliminate liability in certain situations, as long as certain conditions are met. In most cases, encryption of personal data will provide a safe harbor in the event the protected information is stolen.

Reciprocity refers to a mutual recognition between two parties where each enjoys an equal benefit from the relationship. In terms of compliance, reciprocity means that two countries

---

recognize each others regulatory requirements and agree they are adequate to meet the requirements of their own laws.

There was a reciprocal agreement between the US and the EU called the Safe Harbor Framework that basically said a company that complied with their local privacy laws could claim safe harbor if data they had about citizens from another country was breached. On October 16, 2015, that framework was declared invalid by the European Court of Justice because the US laws were inadequate compared to those of the EU.

This created a situation where a US-based organization could be sanctioned in the EU if they possessed personal information about an EU citizen or resident that was breached - even if they were in compliance with US laws.

While this situation has been resolved by the new EU-US Privacy Shield Framework, it illustrates just how difficult compliance can be when multiple privacy laws come into play.

Privacy Shield only applies to data protection and encryption, not the specific requirements of privacy laws. GDPR privacy provisions still apply to all organizations, regardless of location.

A STRUCTURED APPROACH

A security framework is a set of industry standards and best practices to help organizations manage cybersecurity risks, and there are numerous frameworks available to select from. Like many of the things we've talked about so far, frameworks are not a one-size-fits-all approach to managing cybersecurity risk.

Every organization will have unique needs – different threats, different vulnerabilities and weaknesses, and different risk tolerances - and there are different ways to treat all of these. There are some industries that gravitate towards specific frameworks more than others because of these differences. How an organization implements the items within any given framework will also vary. Ultimately, a security framework will help organizations to better manage their cybersecurity risks.

NIST Cybersecurity Framework

NIST published the first version of the *Framework for Improving Critical Infrastructure Cybersecurity* in 2014. Also known as the NIST Cybersecurity Framework, the NIST CSF, or simply the NIST Framework, it was created in response to US Executive Order 13636, which states

> *It is the Policy of the United States to enhance the security and resilience of the Nation's critical infrastructure and to maintain a cyber environment that encourages efficiency, innovation, and economic prosperity while promoting safety, security, business confidentiality, privacy, and civil liberties.*[53]

The *critical infrastructure* in the title refers to 16 industries that the United States Department of Homeland Security (DHS) has identified as being "vital to the country, and that their incapacitation or destruction would have a debilitating effect on security, national economic security, national public health or safety, or any combination thereof."[54]

That may have been the original focus, but it was written in such a way that its usefulness has expanded greatly. In fact, the US Federal Trade Commission (FTC) now recommends that all organizations should adopt the CSF as a best practice. It's been embraced and implemented by organizations of all sizes, and by other countries as well.[55]

There are three primary reasons I recommend the NIST CSF for small businesses, especially if they haven't already adopted a framework.

- It's flexible and can apply to organizations in any industry.
- It's free.
- It cross-references other frameworks.

This last bullet, having cross references, allows you to assess the cybersecurity capabilities of any other organization with which you conduct business.

At this point, you may be asking "Why should I care how other organization's handle their own cybersecurity?"

I'm glad you asked!

Given the nature of the hyperconnected world I've already mentioned, it's nearly impossible to conduct business without computers or the Internet. If you think back to the example of 15 Petals, the breach of that customer's data may have occurred at a supplier that had inadequate cybersecurity practices.

In reality, your organization's cybersecurity is directly tied to that of your supply chain. Their vulnerabilities and weaknesses can have an impact on your organization - just like your security posture can affect them.

The first version of the NIST Framework didn't address cyber risk management of the supply chain. That's been addressed in version 1.1, which was published in April 2018. This update also included sections about disclosing vulnerabilities and allowing organizations to better assess their own cybersecurity risk.

How to use the NIST CSF

The CSF consists of standards, guidelines, and best practices to manage cybersecurity risk. The CSF is technology neutral, meaning it doesn't matter what devices or systems your organization has implemented. Instead, it relies on a variety of existing standards, guidelines, and practices to achieve resilience. The CSF also provides the means to:

- Describe your organization's current cybersecurity posture;
- Describe your organization's target state;
- Identify and prioritize opportunities your organization can take to improve using an iterative and repeatable process;
- Assess the progress you're making towards your target state;
- Effectively communicate about cybersecurity risk.

Despite being a NIST publication, the CSF is not country-specific, as seen with Japan's usage.[56] By also promoting the use of a common vocabulary, the CSF can strengthen cybersecurity efforts and contribute to developing stronger international cooperation on cybersecurity.

Framework Core

The Framework Core is a group of activities and their desired outcomes. It's written to incorporate standards and guidelines in such a way that cybersecurity activities can be communicated in a common way throughout an organization.

As shown in the diagram on the right, the NIST CSF divides cybersecurity into five functions: Identify, Protect, Detect, Respond, and Recover. When taken together, these functions provide a lifecycle view of cybersecurity risk management.

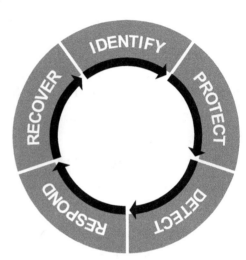

Beneath these functions are various categories and sub-categories that cover the cybersecurity spectrum, plus the cross references I mentioned earlier. The functions, categories, sub-categories, and references comprise the *Framework Core*, which is typically represented in the following manner.

FUNCTION	CATEGORY	SUBCATEGORY	REFERENCES
IDENTIFY			
PROTECT			
DETECT			
RESPOND			
RECOVER			

NIST CSF Functions

Each of the five functions have specific goals associated with them. When taken together, they provide a holistic view of the things organizations should be doing to minimize their risk.

- *Identify*. Create an inventory of systems, devices, assets, data, and capabilities so that your organization knows what you need to protect.
- *Protect*. Implement the countermeasures that your organization needs to ensure the confidentiality, integrity, and availability of critical services.
- *Detect*. Have the ability to identify a cybersecurity event.
- *Respond*. Be able to take actions to stop the bleeding action after a cybersecurity event is confirmed.
- *Recover*. Be able to figure out what the bad guys did in order to restore systems and devices that were impacted, so that you can get back to business.

NIST CSF Categories

There are 24 categories in the CSF. While that may seem daunting, they're broken up in such a way that they're not intimidating. The CSF is designed to walk an organization through its implementation.

NIST also knows that not every organization will be able to tackle the whole thing at once. There's nothing wrong with selecting those things that will be of the greatest benefit to your organization as a starting point. The goal is continuous improvement and moving towards your target state.

In order to give you an idea of what the Framework is all about, I'll briefly describe what each of the categories is trying to determine. I'm not going to dive into the 108 subcategories - there's enough information already available directly from NIST that any organization can freely access and utilize.

The Identify Function Categories

- **Asset Management:** Do you know everything that enables your organization to conduct business? How important is each one to keeping your organization running? Assets include people, systems, devices, and data.
- **Business Environment:** What is your mission statement? What does your organization do? Who are your stakeholders? If something bad happens, what needs to be prioritized?
- **Governance:** Do you have policies and procedures? Do you have regulatory requirements that have to be met?
- **Risk Assessment:** Does your organization have an understanding of how cybersecurity risks can impact your assets, business environment, and governance?
- **Risk Management Strategy:** What is your organization's risk tolerance? What assumptions have been made regarding your priorities and constraints?
- **Supply Chain Risk Management:** Do you know who all of your suppliers are? Is your organization part of someone else's supply chain? If something bad happens, do you know who needs to be notified?

The Protect Function Categories

- **Identity Management, Authentication, and Access Control:** Do you know who has access to your devices and systems? To your buildings? Is everyone's level of access appropriate?
- **Awareness and Training:** Are employees trained on cybersecurity risks? Does everyone know what to do if something bad happens?
- **Data Security:** Is the CIA of your organization's data appropriately managed and protected?
- **Information Protection Processes and Procedures:** Are your policies and procedures maintained and updated? Are there technical controls in place to enforce them?
- **Maintenance:** Are your devices and systems managed per your policies?
- **Protective Technologies:** Are the technical controls your organization has in place managed and monitored? Do they adequately protect the necessary assets to minimize business disruption?

The Detect Function Categories

This function is admittedly more advanced than the others, and assumes that technical controls are in place. Without technical controls and monitoring, however, how will your organization know it's been compromised?

- **Anomalies and Events:** Do you know what normal traffic looks like on your network?
- **Security Continuous Monitoring:** Are you monitoring your devices and systems all the time?

- **Detection Processes:** Are you able to detect abnormal activity quickly in order to minimize impact and damage?

The Respond Function Categories

- **Response Planning:** Do you have a plan in in place should something bad happens? Does everyone within your organization know what to do? Do you have a cybersecurity organization you can contact for assistance?
- **Communications:** Are you able to communicate with your employees? Do you know which law enforcement agencies may need to be contacted? Do you need to inform the media?
- **Analysis:** Are you able to determine what happened? Can you determine how many assets were effected?
- **Mitigation:** Can you stop the attack? Are your existing countermeasures able to mitigate the impact?
- **Improvements:** Are you documenting everything you're doing, so that you'll be better prepared next time?

The Recover Function Categories

- **Recovery Planning:** Do your plans include what's necessary to get your devices and systems functioning again?
- **Improvements:** Do you have a process to incorporate what you've learned back into the NIST CSF cycle?
- **Communications:** Are you able to inform whomever necessary about your recovery efforts? How will you tell your customers that you're back in business?

CONTINUING THE JOURNEY

I know I've thrown a lot of information at you pretty quickly and I've done my best to keep the geek-speak out of it. Remember that cybersecurity is a journey, not a destination. The resources in this chapter are intended to supplement what I've shared in this book and to help you move along that journey.

Information I've directly referenced, whether for statistics, history, or to support my positions on various topics, can be found in the Endnotes. But a good percentage of those references won't be relevant when building your organization's cybersecurity plan.

I've got good news though. This chapter is all about providing sources where you can find more information on the topics contained in the book.

Informational Resources for Small Business

There is a surprising amount of information about cybersecurity for small business you can find on the Internet. However, I've limited the links in this section to those from US Government organizations. One of the main reasons is because all of the information is free and available to everyone.

There are obviously many other resources available by simply searching the Internet. Regardless of which sources you select, always do what's best for your organization, because you know it better than anyone.

Small Business Administration

There are several good resources available from the SBA. The first is a 30 minute self-paced training program. While aimed at business owners, it has content that may be beneficial for all employees. It can be found at the link below.

< *https://www.sba.gov/course/cybersecurity-small-businesses/* >

Additional information can be found in a cybersecurity landing page. From here, there are links to additional SBA resources.

< *https://www.sba.gov/managing-business/cybersecurity* >

Federal Trade Commission

The FTC has two main goals: protect consumers and promote competition. It has a broad oversight role that allows them to investigate and fine organization that are out of compliance.

However, they also have extensive resources available to help organizations from running afoul of laws and regulations.

Knowing that cybersecurity can be a difficult topic, the FTC has put together a program they refer to as *Start with Security*.
< *https://www.ftc.gov/tips-advice/business-center/guidance/start-security-guide-business* >

It includes the ubiquitous top ten list, but this one provides more information. Not only does each item have a corresponding video, there are also examples of enforcement actions the FTC has taken - so that you can better protect your organization.

The FTC has a broader guide for protecting small businesses that also discussed scams that target smaller organizations and what to do in the event of a breach.
< *https://www.ftc.gov/tips-advice/business-center/small-businesses* >

National Institute of Standards and Technology
NIST's mission is very broad, so it can be difficult to find relevant information on the website. I've dedicated an entire chapter to the NIST Cybersecurity Framework, but you can find additional information on their website.
< *https://www.nist.gov/cyberframework* >

There's also a stand-alone guide from NIST entitled *Small Business Information Security: The Fundamentals* that has tools to help organizations get a better handle on risk.

< *https://doi.org/10.6028/NIST.IR.7621r1* >

US Computer Emergency Response Team

The US-CERT offers some basic information under the heading of *Critical Infrastructure*. The section can be misleading, however, because the information can be useful to any organization. The Cybersecurity Resources Road Map (CRR) is a good way to quickly ascertain your organizations cyber maturity.

< *https://www.us-cert.gov/ccubedvp/smb* >

Stop. Think. Connect.

Stop. Think. Connect. is a Department of Homeland Security program to better educate consumers about cybersecurity, but it also has resources for small businesses. The information here can easily be used to create cybersecurity awareness within your organization.

< *https://www.dhs.gov/publication/stopthinkconnect-small-business-resources* >

Stay Safe Online

This is another site with a consumer focus but that also has information valuable for smaller organizations. While not actually a government site, they partner with Stop. Think. Connect. and have a program called *CyberSecure My Business* that uses the NIST CSF as it's foundation.

< *https://staysafeonline.org/* >

Get Involved

While reading information in books and online can be a great way to learn about cybersecurity, some individuals prefer face-to-face interactions with their peers. Good news! There are numerous membership organizations and alliances that can help in that regard, too.

Internet Security Alliance
There are lot of large organizations that are members of the ISA, which can be both helpful and intimidating at the same time. And ISA does require organizations that join to have some financial skin the game. Associate Membership for smaller organizations have an annual cost of $5000, which may put this out of reach for many organizations.

Information Systems Security Association International
Knows as ISSA, they specialize in connecting cybersecurity professionals through various chapters across the US and the world. They are a membership organization and not focused specifically on small business, but they have resources that may be of interest. General memberships are roughly $130, but vary because of differences in local chapter dues.

ISACA
This is another membership organization focused on information security, but they offer a number of certifications and education. They also created the COBIT framework. Annual membership are roughly $200, but also vary based on local dues.

InfraGard

A public-private partnership between the FBI and members in the private sector, InfraGard members include business executives, entrepreneurs, law enforcement, academia, computer geeks, and many others. There are local chapters throughout the US, most of whom have regular meetings to discuss regionally-specific topics. InfraGard memberships are for individuals, not organizations, and require a vetting process.

The Stuff I Read

Last, but certainly not least, this section lists some of cybersecurity books that I find fascinating and the reason why. Any of these would be great additions to your cybersecurity library.

Crypto - Steven Levy

Crypto is a fascinating look at how modern cryptography came to be. It's the story of cyber freedom fighters taking on the government to ensure privacy on the Internet.

Beyond Fear - Bruce Schneier

Schneier argues that everyone needs to have a better understanding of security. How can we make informed decisions if we don't understand what our choices really are? *Beyond Fear* offers a common sense approach that I appreciate.

Data and Goliath - Bruce Schneier

One of the most recent books by Schneier, *Data and Goliath* looks at the world of data collection and aggregation. Facebook is notorious for its data analytics, but website trackers and beacons collect more than most people realize.

The Art of Invisibility - Kevin Mitnick
You could consider *The Art of Invisibility* to be the guide for protecting yourself from the world described in *Data and Goliath*. Mitnick shows some simple techniques and advanced concepts to protect your privacy and make yourself as anonymous as possible.

Future Crimes - Marc Goodman
Taking the reader into the underbelly of the Internet, *Future Crimes* reinforces how cybercriminals weaponize devices and systems for their own purposes.

Glass Houses - Joel Brenner
Brenner has some unique insights in the world of cybersecurity from his time with the NSA. *Glass Houses* explores what you can (and more importantly, can't) do to protect ourselves from cybercriminals.

Linchpin - Seth Godin
Okay, this one isn't a book about cybersecurity. But it does take a look at how a person can make a significant impact, for themselves, their organization, or of society as a whole. You just have to be willing to take that next step.

I'm hopeful that *Protecting Your Assets* will help you take that next step for your organization. Small businesses are the backbone of the global economy - and it's time organizations use that knowledge and power to their advantage.

GLOSSARY

Analog	Generally refers to things that don't require devices and systems, e.g. not digital. Example: a pen and paper is the analog equivalent of a computer tablet and stylus.
Anonymity	Freedom from Identification.
Application	A task-specific piece of software that runs within an operating system. Word processors, spreadsheets, and databases are examples of applications.
Asset	Anything of value to an organization.
Attacker	Refer to Cybercriminal.
Authentication	The process of proving your identity to systems or devices, typically with a user name and password.

Authorization	The level of access and permissions granted to a user once they have successfully authenticated to a system or device.
Availability	Ensuring that information can be accessed whenever it's needed.
Bad Guy	Refer to Cybercriminal.
BCP	Refer to Business Continuity Planning.
Beacon	Similar to trackers, beacons monitor activity and collect information about visitors to a website and their computers.
Botnet	A group of devices and systems infected with malware and controlled by cybercriminals. The combined computing power is used to attack other devices and systems for various nefarious purposes.
Breach	A successful attack against a device or system that allowed unauthorized individuals to access and steal information.
Brute Force	An inelegant method used by cybercriminals to try and break into devices and systems using trial-and-error to guess passwords or other authentication information.
Business Continuity Planning	The process of identifying potential risks faced by an organization and developing a response plan to deal those risks should they be realized.
Business Resumption	Refer to Disaster Recovery.
CCPA	Refer to California Consumer Privacy Act.

Cloud	Refer to Cloud Computing.
Cloud Computing	Typically referred to simply as "The Cloud", Cloud Computing is the concept of utilizing leased systems and devices housed in a physically different location and accessed though the Internet.
Compliance	Conforming to regulatory or industry-specific requirements.
Confidentiality	Ensuring that only authorized individuals have access to information, and inadvertent disclosure is prevented.
Countermeasure	Actions taken to minimize the impact of a threat.
Cryptography	The art of creating and solving (or breaking) codes. It's the genesis of the words Encryption and Decryption.
Cybercriminal	An individual or organization that uses systems, devices, and the Internet to attack other systems and devices for financial gain.
Cybersecurity	The practice of protecting devices and systems, and the information they contain, from being attacked, stolen, or compromised.
Decryption	The process of converting a file from an encrypted state back into human-readable format.
Device	Devices are physical objects with a processor, operating system, and user interface. Servers, personal computers, tablets, and smartphones are different types of devices.

Digital Business	An organization that uses technology as a competitive advantage for all of its operations.
Disaster Planning	Refer to Business Continuity Planning.
Disaster Recovery	The implementation of the BCP after something has happed to disrupt an organization's business, with the goal of returning to normal as quickly as possible.
Disrupter	A new innovation or business model that goes against entrenched or established industries, or creates an entirely new market.
DR	Refer to Disaster Recovery.
Encryption	The process of converting information from a human-readable format to a format that is not usable without the appropriate key.
Encryption Key	A very long sequence of characters used to encrypt a document or file.
Factor	Derived from the mathematical concept of numbers that are multiplied together, factors are the different components that must be possessed (and ultimately combined) in order to prove identity to systems or devices.
FUDGE	Short for Fear, Uncertainty, Doubt, Generalities, and Exaggerations. These are tactics used to attempt to unrealistically or unnecessarily frighten individuals about cybersecurity dangers.
GDPR	Refer to General Data Protection Regulation.

General Data Protection Regulation	Typically referred to as GDPR, the General Data Protection Regulation is a European Union law designed to protect the privacy of EU residents and citizens. While if covers numerous privacy topics, the most well known is the "right to be forgotten".
GLBA	Refer to Gramm-Leach-Bliley Act.
Gramm-Leach-Bliley Act	Typically referred to as GLBA, the official name is the Financial Services Modernization Act of 1999. GLBA is a US federal law governing financial institutions and their collection, disclosure, and protection of customer PII (among other provisions).
Health Information Technology for Economic and Clinical Health Act	Typically referred to as HITECH, this US law governs privacy in the health care industry. Enacted in 2009, it promoted electronic health records, partnered with NIST to created technology standards, and built on HIPAA's privacy rules to require breach notifications.
Health Insurance Portability and Accountability Act	Typically referred to as HIPAA, this US law reformed the healthcare industry when it was passed in 1999. Consisting of five titles, Title II's "Privacy Rule" is the best known and established standards for data safeguarding and giving individual's access to their own PHI records.
HIPAA	Refer to Health Insurance Portability and Accountability Act.
HITECH	Refer to Health Information Technology for Economic and Clinical Health Act.

Glossary

Identity | The unique information associated with an individual. From the systems and devices standpoint, Identity relates to the permissions assigned to a user profile.

Impact | The effect on an organization if a threat exploits a vulnerability or weakness.

In the Wild | Term to describe something on the open Internet, not in a research context, that hasn't been contained or controlled.

Integrity | Ensuring that information is true and accurate, that any changes are authorized, and that controls are in place to prevent or detect unauthorized changes.

Internet | A global network interconnecting systems and devices, allowing for realtime communications and collaboration. Originally conceived by the US Defense Advanced Research Projects Agency in the 1960s, the Internet has become a critical tool for conducting business.

Jailbreak | Gaining system level access to a device for the purpose of circumventing controls put in place by the manufacturer.

Keylogger | A type of malware that captures keyboard input from systems it has infected. The information captured includes everything the individual types, including user names and passwords, is then sent back to an attacker.

Law	A systems of rules that define proper behavior or procedures in order to regulate the actions of individuals or organizations, typically issues by a governing body such as state or federal governments.
Least Priviledge	The principle of only having enough permissions on devices and systems to complete your required tasks.
Malware	A combination of the words Malicious Software, malware include several categories of applications designed to harm any system on which it runs.
Modem	Short for a Modulation/Demodulation, it's a device that allows different systems to connect to each other. In modern usage, it's the device that allows Internet connectivity.
National Institute of Standards and Technology	Typically referred to as NIST, the National Institute of Standards and Technology is a US Government organization underneath the US Department of Commerce. Their mission is "to promote U.S. innovation and industrial competitiveness by advancing measurement science, standards, and technology in ways that enhance economic security and improve our quality of life."
NIST	Refer to National Institute of Standards and Technology.
NIST CSF	Refer to NIST Cybersecurity Framework.

NIST Cybersecurity Framework	Typically referred to as the NIST CSF or simply the NIST Framework, the NIST Cybersecurity Framework was created by presidential order in 2013. It offers guidance to document, understand, and reduce cybersecurity risk.
Operating System	Software used to interact with the hardware resource of a device, such as the keyboard, mouse, monitor, storage, and memory.
Payment Card Industry	Typically shortened to PCI, the Payment Card Industry includes any organization that issues, collects, processes, or transmits debit and credit card information.
PCI	Refer to Payment Card Industry.
PCI Data Security Standard	Typically shortened to PCI DSS. Published by the PCI SSC, the Data Safeguarding Standard is the minimum set of requirements that an organization must adhere to. Failure to comply with the DSS can result in an organization no longer being allowed to accept or process debit and credit cards.
PCI DSS	Refer to PCI Data Security Standard.
PCI Security Standards Council	Typically shortened to PCI SSC, the Security Standards Council is responsible for developing and enforcing minimum standards for the safe handling of debit and credit card information.
PCI SSC	Refer to PCI Security Standards Council.

Personally Identifiable Information	Typically shortened to PII, it is nonpublic information that that can be used to locate, or identify an individual. What constitutes PII differs by country. Since the United States lacks a federal privacy law, the definitions vary by state.
PHI	Refer to Protected Health Information.
PII	Refer to Personally Identifiable Information.
Privacy	Freedom from Observation.
Private Data	Refer to Personally Identifiable Information.
Protected Health Information	Typically shortened to PHI, Protected Health Information is defined under US law as information regarding the diagnosis, care, and treatment of a condition that can be linked back to an individual.
Rainbow Table	A database of all possible combinations of upper and lower case letters, numbers, and special character used by cybercriminals to try and passwords in a system.
Ransomware	A type of malware that encrypts information on systems it has infected. In order to retrieve the information, users of infected devices are instructed to pay a ransom for the decryption key - which is where the name comes from.
Regulation	A rule or directive made and enforced by an executive authority or enforcement agency and having the force of law.

Risk	The threat posed to an organization based on potential threats, the impact if that threat is realized, and the likelihood of it happening.
Security	Freedom from Danger.
Special Character	Non-alpha, non-numeric characters on computer keyboards, including quotes, brackets, braces, periods, comma, all the characters above the number keys, and numerous others.
Spyware	A type of malware designed to capture information about individuals or organizations from systems or devices it has infected. Spyware is typically used for reconnaissance as part of a larger attack.
System	The combination of devices, operating systems, and applications used to perform a task.
Threat	External factors that can impact a system's confidentiality, integrity, or availability.
Tracker	Small pieces of computer code used on some websites to track user behaviors and interactions.
Virus	A type of malware that infects computers in order to gather information, steal data, or cause damage to applications or operating systems.
Vulnerability	A systemic weakness within a device or system that can be exploited.

Weakness   A deficiency in the implementation or configuration of a device or system that can be exploited.

Widget   Small pieces of pre-written computer code that perform a specific function on a webpage, such as showing advertisements.

ENDNOTES

[1] Cate Rushton, "The History of Amazon.com", Techwalla, accessed December 2018. https://www.techwalla.com/articles/the-history-of-amazoncom

[2] Amazon.com, Inc. 2017 Annual Report, published February 1, 2018, p. 32, accessed December 2018. https://ir.aboutamazon.com/static-files/917130c5-e6bf-4790-a7bc-cc43ac7fb30a

[3] "Glossary", *Komprise*, accessed December 2018, https://www.komprise.com/glossary_terms/digital-business/

[4] Verizon Enterprise, *2018 Data Breach Investigation Report (11th Edition)*, p5.

[5] Steve Morgan, "2017 Cybercrime Report", *Cybersecurity Ventures*, accessed December 2018. https://cybersecurityventures.com/2015-wp/wp-content/uploads/2017/10/2017-Cybercrime-Report.pdf

[6] Tony Bradley, "Cybercrime is the Modern-Day Mafia", *Forbes Online*, published October 16, 2015; accessed December 2018. https://www.forbes.com/sites/tonybradley/2015/10/16/cybercrime-is-the-modern-day-mafia/#401371eb4539

[7] Brian Krebs, "Who Makes the IoT Things Under Attack?", *Krebs on Security*, published October 3, 2016; accessed December 2018. https://krebsonsecurity.com/2016/10/who-makes-the-iot-things-under-attack/

[8] James Veitch, "The agony of trying to unsubscribe", *TED Talks*, accessed December 2018. https://en.tiny.ted.com/talks/james_veitch_the_agony_of_trying_to_unsubscribe

[9] Verizon Enterprise, *2018 Report*, p5.

[10] SBA Office of Advocacy, *Frequently Asked Questions About Small Business*, (US Small Business Administration), published August 2018; accessed September 2018. https://www.sba.gov/sites/default/files/advocacy/Frequently-Asked-Questions-Small-Business-2018.pdf

[11] *Statistical Release*, (Department of Business, Energy & Industrial Strategy, October 11, 2018); accessed December 2018. https://assets.publishing.service.gov.uk/government/uploads/system/uploads/attachment_data/file/746599/OFFICIAL_SENSITIVE_-_BPE_2018_-_statistical_release_FINAL_FINAL.pdf

[12] Celia Paulsen and Patricia Toth, *Small Business Information Security: The Fundamentals* (National Institute of Standards and Technology document NISTIR 7621 Revision 1: November 2016), p. 1. https://doi.org/10.6028/NIST.IR.7621r1

[13] "What is an SME?", *European Commission> Internal Market, Industry, Entrepreneurship and SMEs,* accessed November 2018, http://ec.europa.eu/growth/smes/business-friendly-environment/sme-definition_en

[14] Chris Rhodes, *BRIEFING PAPER Number 06152, 12 December 2018*, (House of Commons Library, 2018), accessed December 2018. https://researchbriefings.files.parliament.uk/documents/SN06152/SN06152.pdf

[15] Target Corporation 2016 Annual Report, published March 8, 2017, p. 44, accessed December 2018. https://corporate.target.com/_media/TargetCorp/annualreports/2016/pdfs/Target-2016-Annual-Report.pdf

[16] Brian Krebs, "Inside Target Corp., Days After 2013 Breach", Krebs on Security, last modified September 21, 2015; accessed October 2018. https://krebsonsecurity.com/2015/09/inside-target-corp-days-after-2013-breach/

[17] John Hall, "SplashData's Top 100 Worst Passwords of 2018", *TeamsID,* last modified December 13, 2018; accessed December 2018. https://www.teamsid.com/splashdatas-top-100-worst-passwords-of-2018/

18 Morgan Slain, "A Brief History of the Password Problem, Part 3: Worst Passwords of 2013", *TeamsID*, last modified December 2013; accessed December 2018. https://www.teamsid.com/worst-passwords-of-2013/

19 Morgan Slain, "A short history of passwords", *SplashID Blog*, last modified January 7, 2016; accessed November 2018. http://blog.splashid.com/a-short-history-of-passwords/

20 Randall Munroe, "Password Strength", xkcd, published August 10, 2011; accessed October 2018. https://xkcd.com/936/

21 "936: Password Strength", *explain xkcd wiki*, last updated October 31, 2018; accessed November 2018. https://www.explainxkcd.com/wiki/index.php/936:_Password_Strength

22 Ryan Francis, "Vendors approve of NIST password draft", *CSO Online*, last update May 9, 2017; accessed December 2018. https://www.csoonline.com/article/3195181/data-protection/vendors-approve-of-nist-password-draft.html

23 "factor", *Merriam-Webster Online*, accessed December 2018. https://www.merriam-webster.com/dictionary/factor

24 *The FIDO Alliance*, accessed December 2018. https://fidoalliance.org/

25 "FIDO Members", *The FIDO Alliance*, accessed December 2018. *https://fidoalliance.org/members/*

26 "FIDO Certified Showcase", *The FIDO Alliance*, accessed December 2018. https://fidoalliance.org/fido-certified-showcase/

27 "First Instance of Actual Computer Bug Being Found", *The Computer History Museum*, accessed August 2018. http://www.computerhistory.org/tdih/september/9/

28 *Common Vulnerabilities and Exposures database*. https://cve.mitre.org/

29 "CVE-2002-0649", *NIST National Vulnerabilities Database*, last modified October 19, 2018; accessed November 2018. https://nvd.nist.gov/vuln/detail/CVE-2002-0649

30 "Operating System by Version", *NetMarketShare.com*, report generated December 31, 2018.

31 "The Creeper Worm, the First Computer Virus", *History of Information*, accessed December 2018. http://www.historyofinformation.com/detail.php?entryid=2860

32 John von Neumann and Arthur W. Burks, *Theory of Self-Reproducing Automata*. (1966, University of Illinois Press, Urbana, IL.)

33 "ILOVEYOU Virus", *TechTarget*, last modified February 2006; accessed October 2018. https://searchsecurity.techtarget.com/definition/ILOVEYOU-virus

34 "Malware Statistics, Total Malware", *AV-Test*, accessed December 2018. https://www.av-test.org/en/statistics/malware/

35 Robert Siciliano, "Security Awareness Training is Essential for Small Business", *Entrepreneur*, last updated February 27, 2017; accessed October 2018. https://www.entrepreneur.com/article/282990

[36] Alan Lakein, *How to Get Control of Your Time and Your Life*, p. 25. (1973, New American Library, New York, NY.)

[37] James A. Martin, "Planning averts disaster for L.A. bond trading firm", *Computerworld*, May 9, 1988, p. 4.

[38] Paul Coleman, "The First Interstate Bank Fire", *Disaster Recovery Journal*, last updated October 29, 2007; accessed October 2018. https://www.drj.com/drj-world-archives/fires/the-first-interstate-bank-fire.html

[39] "Browser Market Share", *NetMarketShare.com*, report generated December 31, 2018.

[40] The How-To Geek, *Is Hiding Your Wireless SSID Really More Secure?*, Lifehacker, last updates September 13, 2010; accessed December 2018. https://lifehacker.com/5636856/is-hiding-your-wireless-ssid-really-more-secure

[41] Steve Riley, "Myth vs. reality: Wireless SSIDs", *Microsoft TechNet*, last updated October 16, 2007; accessed December 2018. https://blogs.technet.microsoft.com/steriley/2007/10/16/myth-vs-reality-wireless-ssids/

42 CVE-2013-13077", *NIST National Vulnerabilities Database*, last modified November 13, 2018; accessed December 2018.https://nvd.nist.gov/vuln/detail/CVE-2017-13077

[43] Christian Moldes, "Compliant but not Secure: Why PCI-Certified Companies Are Being Breached", *CSIAC Journal, Volume 6, Number 1* (May 2018). pp. 18-24.

44 "Privacy Laws by Country", *PrivacyPolicies.com,* accessed December 2018. https://privacypolicies.com/blog/privacy-law-by-country/

45 *General Data Protection Regulation*, preamble (1)

46 ibid., Article 4 (1)

47 ibid., Article 17

48 Claudio R Barbosa and Pedro Vilhena, "Data Protection in Brazil: Overview", *Thomson Reuters Practical Law*, last updated December 1, 2018; accessed December 2018. https://content.next.westlaw.com/4-520-1732?transitionType=Default&contextData=(sc.Default)&__lrTS=20190120014022984&firstPage=true&bhcp=1#co_anchor_a254967

49 Katie Yahnke, "A Practical Guide to Data Privacy Laws by Country", *i-Sight*, accessed December 2018. https://i-sight.com/resources/a-practical-guide-to-data-privacy-laws-by-country/U.S.

50 *California Consumer Privacy Act of 2018*, Section 4.5 (7) (c)

51 ibid. Section 3, item 1798-140 (1)

52 *Tennessee Code Annotated*, §47-18-2107(a)(4)

53 Barack Obama, "Executive Order 13636", issued February 12, 2013; accessed December 2018. https://obamawhitehouse.archives.gov/the-press-office/2013/02/12/executive-order-improving-critical-infrastructure-cybersecurity

54 "Critical Infrastructure Sectors", *US Department of Homeland Security*, accessed July 2018. https://www.dhs.gov/cisa/critical-infrastructure-sectors

[55] "Success Story: Japanese Cross-Sector Forum", *NIST*, last updated October 19, 2018; accessed October 2018. https://www.nist.gov/node/1332326/japanese-cross-sector-forum

[56] ibid.

About the Author

John A. Schaefer is a computer geek with over 30 years of experience in information technology, with a focus on cybersecurity. He's been doing this for so long, in fact, that cybersecurity wasn't even a word when he started.

John isn't your typical geek, though. Having spent the majority of his professional career working for Fortune 50 companies, he knows that geek-speak doesn't go over very well in the boardroom. He has a rare ability for geeks: to explain complex technical information in ways that non-geeks can understand.

He's been quoted in PC Week and The Wall Street Journal for some of his past projects, and was recently a guest speaker for a graduate level computer science class at Vanderbilt University.

Talking to small business owners, John realized there's a need that's not being met for cybersecurity information. It's this void that led John to start Eastvale Cyber.

Focused exclusively on small businesses and providing the information they need to improve their security without spending a fortune, John's goal is for Eastvale Cyber to become the most trusted source of cybersecurity information for small businesses.

www.ingramcontent.com/pod-product-compliance
Lightning Source LLC
La Vergne TN
LVHW052302060326
832902LV00021B/3681